To Eddy Spaghetti Rabe and to the PAWS
(Pet Animal Welfare Society) Shelter of
Norwalk, Connecticut, for helping us make
him a beloved member of our family
—T.R.

The editors would like to thank
BARBARA KIEFER, Ph.D.,
Charlotte S. Huck Professor of Children's Literature,
The Ohio State University, and
STEPHEN L. ZAWISTOWSKI, Ph.D., CAAB,
Adjunct Professor of Clinical Medicine,
University of Illinois College of Veterinary Medicine,
for their assistance in the preparation of this book.

Visit us on the Web!
randomhouse.com/kids
Seussville.com

Educators and librarians, for a variety of teaching tools, visit us at
RHTeachersLibrarians.com

Library of Congress Cataloging-in-Publication Data
Rabe, Tish.
What cat is that? : all about cats / by Tish Rabe ; illustrated by Aristides Ruiz and
Joe Mathieu. — First edition.
    pages   cm. — (The cat in the hat's learning library)
Audience: 5–8.
Summary: "The Cat in the Hat learns all about cats—wild and domestic—in this feline-focused
Cat in the Hat's Learning Library book." — Provided by publisher.
ISBN 978-0-375-86640-1 (trade) — ISBN 978-0-375-96640-8 (lib. bdg.)
1. Cats—Juvenile literature. I. Ruiz, Aristides, illustrator. II. Mathieu, Joe, 1949– illustrator.
III. Title.
QL737.C23R245 2013 599.75—dc23 2013002984

Printed in the United States of America 10 9 8 7 6 5 4 3 2 1 First Edition

What Cat Is That?

by Tish Rabe

illustrated by Aristides Ruiz and Joe Mathieu

The Cat in the Hat's Learning Library®

Random House 🏠 New York

I'm the Cat in the Hat.
Let us leave right away
to see all the cats
we can see in one day.

We'll meet lions in Kenya,
tigers in Bangkok,
snow leopards in China,
Siamese down the block.

In my Kitty-Cat-Copter
we'll travel around
to all different places
where cats can be found!

Cats are mammals that have scratchy tongues, padded paws, sensitive whiskers, and very sharp claws.

Cats like to chase, pounce, eat, wrestle, and hide. Some cats live indoors. Some cats live outside.

Here's a fact about cats
I did not know before:
Some can roar but can't purr.
Some can purr but can't roar!

Tigers are the biggest.
They hunt in the night.
Most are orange with black stripes
and patches of white.

Ocelots, like this one,
are cats that are rare.
Go to a rain forest.
You might find one there.

Leopards are strong,
and as you can see,
a leopard can quickly
climb up a tree.

Some cats are wild,
like the ones we just met.
A domesticated cat
can be kept as a pet.

Persians have long fur,
and I'd like to mention,
their long, silky coats
need a lot of attention.

Siamese have short fur,
and I can hear now,
this kind of cat makes
a mournful "meow."

Do cats like to swim?
You may think "No way,"
but Turkish swimming cats
like to get wet and play!

Cats need to scratch to take care of their paws. When they scratch, they are pulling dead skin off their claws.

SNOW LEOPARD

Cats' claws are strong. Here's another cat fact: Cats' claws can extend. They can also retract.

Extend means to push out.

Retract means to pull in.

Cats' claws pull into sheaths, which are pockets of skin.

Cheetahs' claws don't retract. They run fast and must grip the ground with their claws so their paws will not slip.

COUGAR

Cats have flexible spines.
This is one reason why
cats can stretch really long
or arch their backs high.

Cats have small collarbones,
which can move so cats fit
through small spaces, like doors
opened up just a bit.

16

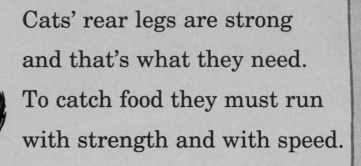

Cats' rear legs are strong
and that's what they need.
To catch food they must run
with strength and with speed.

SERVAL

Cats need their whiskers
and use them each day.
Like your fingertips, whiskers
help cats find their way.

Whiskers help cats
know which way they are going,
if it's cold out or hot,
and which way the wind's blowing.

OCELOT

Cats use their whiskers
each time they explore.

"Is this hard, smooth, or rough?"

"Can I fit through this door?"

Cats can have different markings—
stripes, patches, or spots.
Some cats have few markings
and others have lots.

This tiger has black stripes,
an orange-red coat,
white fur on its belly,
chest, muzzle, and throat.

This cat is white with colored patches, and that is how I know she is a calico cat.

This clouded leopard told me she is proud that each of her spots looks a bit like a cloud.

Cats are active at dawn
and again at twilight.
For this reason, they see
very well in dim light.

In dim light, cats' pupils
grow round and wide.
This lets their eyes get
the most light inside.

Look at a cat's eyes
when the light is bright.
Its pupils get narrow
so they let in less light.

MARGAY

Cells in back of their eyes
reflect light, and so
a cat's eyes at night
let off a bright glow!

Cats have different ears.
A Scottish fold cat
has ears that can bend
and are folded and flat.

CARACAL

SAND CAT

I just met these cats—
a boy and a girl.
They're American curl cats
and their ears can curl.

When a cat hears a noise,
its ears turn around,
so each ear can focus
on one single sound.

A cat's nose is wet, and here's one reason why— it picks up smells better than one that is dry.

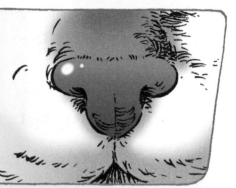

Cats are carnivores, which means they eat meat.

CAT FOOD

THING 2

They taste sour, bitter, and salty but cannot taste sweet.

TASTE BUDS

TASTE BUDS

TASTE BUDS

TASTE BUDS

Cats have sharp teeth
to tear meat and bite.
Some use their teeth
when they get in a fight.

BOBCATS

When a cat is upset,
it might roar or growl.
When a cat is angry,
it might start to howl.

When a cat is threatened,
it might act like this—
it arches its back
and lets out a loud hiss.

A dog wags its tail
when it's excited or glad.
A cat twitches its tail
when it's nervous or mad.

Thing One looked up cat words
and here is the scoop:
What is a clowder?
It's cats in a group!

CLOWDER

When cats rub their cheeks, they leave scent on each other. This tiger cub's leaving her scent on her mother.

This lion is rubbing a tree with his face. His scent tells other cats, "I have been at this place."

When a cat starts to circle
and bumps into you,
leaving its scent,
as Tarzee likes to do . . .

this is called "bunting."
Cats do this, you see,
as their way of saying
"You belong to me."

Cats don't bathe or shower,
but they have a trick.
A cat takes a front paw
and gives it a lick.

It sweeps the wet paw
over its head, and then
it takes the same paw
and licks it again.

Spines on a cat's tongue
help it work like a scraper.
They're rough, and they make
the tongue feel like sandpaper.

Thing Two has a new cat.
He's called Mr. Pickles.
When he licks you, his tongue
is so rough that it tickles!

When wild cats have babies,
mother cats stay alert
to make sure that their
little cubs don't get hurt.

Mother lion keeps her cubs
right by her side.
They blend in with the grass,
and that helps them to hide.

A tiger must raise
her cubs all alone.
In a few years her cubs
will go off on their own.

She licks her cubs
as a sign of affection.
It's her job to find food
and give them protection.

Now I would like
to take you to meet
a litter of kittens
that live down the street.

Born with no teeth
and with eyes that are blue,
these sweet little kittens
are glad to meet you.

Newborn kittens are helpless.
They depend on their mother.
In a few weeks they'll start
to play with each other.

What is a kindle?
Hold on to your socks.
It's a group of kittens,
like these in this box.

KINDLE

When a cat moves her baby,
she carefully holds
the skin on its neck
where it hangs in loose folds.

It won't hurt a kitty
to be moved by its mother
by the scruff of its neck
from one place to another.

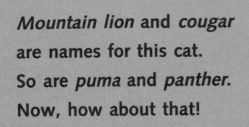

Mountain lion and cougar
are names for this cat.
So are *puma* and *panther*.
Now, how about that!

Kittens grow quickly
and, as you see here,
a kitten grows into
a cat in one year.

Cats live just about
anywhere that you go—
cities, rain forests,
mountains covered in snow.

Cats like to sleep,
and most cats sleep a lot—
on the ground, in a tree,
in a warm, sunny spot.

So now I am sure
cats are taking a nap
all over the world
and right here . . .

. . . in your lap.

GLOSSARY

Calico: Having fur with multi-colored patches.

Collarbone: A curved bone that supports the shoulder.

Cubs: The young of certain animals, such as lions, tigers, and bears.

Domesticated: Tamed, meaning that an animal is comfortable with people and can't live in the wild.

Flexible: Bending easily.

Focus: To direct one's attention to a single thing.

Litter: A group of babies born at the same time to one mother.

Muzzle: The part of an animal's head that includes the mouth and nose.

Pounce: To swoop down on something suddenly.

Pupil: The black part in the center of the eye, which is a hole that lets in light.

Scruff: The back of the neck.

Threatened: In danger.

Twilight: The period of dim light before sunset.

FOR FURTHER READING

Big Cats by Seymour Simon (HarperCollins). Illustrated with photographs, this is an award-winning book about big wild cats—including lions, tigers, leopards, jaguars, cheetahs, pumas, and snow leopards. For ages 5–8.

Cats vs. Dogs by Elizabeth Carney (National Geographic *Kids Readers,* Level 3). A lively comparison of cats and dogs—their ancestors, senses, social lives, and more. For ages 6–8.

Discover Maine Coon Cats by Trudy Micco (Enslow Publishers, *Discover Cats with the Cat Fanciers' Association*). All about the history of Maine coon cats and how to care for them. Other books in the *Discover Cats* series are about Abyssinian, Oriental shorthair, Persian, ragdoll, and mixed-breed cats. For kindergarten–grade 3.

Learning to Care for a Cat by Felicia Lowenstein Niven (Enslow Publishers, *Beginning Pet Care with American Humane*). A simple guide to cat pet care, written with the help of an expert from the American Humane Association. For grades 3–4.

INDEX

Look for these other Green Light Readers
in affordably priced paperbacks and hardcovers!

Level 1/Kindergarten–Grade 1

The Big, Big Wall
Reginald Howard
Illustrated by Ariane Dewey and Jose Aruego

Big Brown Bear
David McPhail

Big Pig and Little Pig
David McPhail

Cloudy Day/Sunny Day
Donald Crews

Come Here, Tiger
Alex Moran
Illustrated by Lisa Campbell Ernst

Down on the Farm
Rita Lascaro

Just Clowning Around
Steven MacDonald
Illustrated by David McPhail

Lost!
Patti Trimble
Illustrated by Daniel Moreton

Popcorn
Alex Moran
Illustrated by Betsy Everitt

Rabbit and Turtle Go to School
Lucy Floyd
Illustrated by Christopher Denise

Rip's Secret Spot
Kristi T. Butler
Illustrated by Joe Cepeda

Sam and Jack
Alex Moran
Illustrated by Tim Bowers

Six Silly Foxes
Alex Moran
Illustrated by Keith Baker

Sometimes
Keith Baker

The Tapping Tale
Judy Giglio
Illustrated by Joe Cepeda

What Day Is It?
Patti Trimble
Illustrated by Daniel Moreton

What I See
Holly Keller

Level 2/Grades 1–2

Animals on the Go
Jessica Brett
Illustrated by Richard Cowdrey

A Bed Full of Cats
Holly Keller

Catch Me If You Can!
Bernard Most

The Chick That Wouldn't Hatch
Claire Daniel
Illustrated by Lisa Campbell Ernst

Daniel's Mystery Egg
Alma Flor Ada
Illustrated by G. Brian Karas

Digger Pig and the Turnip
Caron Lee Cohen
Illustrated by Christopher Denise

The Fox and the Stork
Gerald McDermott

Get That Pest!
Erin Douglas
Illustrated by Wong Herbert Yee

I Wonder
Tana Hoban

Marco's Run
Wesley Cartier
Illustrated by Reynold Ruffins

The Purple Snerd
Rozanne Lanczak Williams
Illustrated by Mary GrandPré

Shoe Town
Janet Stevens and Susan Stevens Crummel
Illustrated by Janet Stevens

Splash!
Ariane Dewey and Jose Aruego

Tumbleweed Stew
Susan Stevens Crummel
Illustrated by Janet Stevens

The Very Boastful Kangaroo
Bernard Most

Why the Frog Has Big Eyes
Betsy Franco
Illustrated by Joung Un Kim

Green Light Readers
For the new reader who's ready to GO!

From Egg to Frog

1. Egg

2. Tadpole

3. Frog

The frog is also fast!
It eats lots of bugs.

Watch out fly!
Mmmm!

Hop, hop!

The frog is big and strong.
It can hop to find food or
run from danger.

At last the tail is gone.
The tadpole is now a
full-grown frog.

Small front legs form next.
The tadpole is almost a frog,
but it still has a tail.

A tadpole has to swim
fast or a fish will eat it.

Soon the tadpole grows two
strong back legs. They help it
to kick and swim fast.

It looks for plants in the pond.
It eats the plants and grows very fast.

At first, the tadpole has a long
tail and a big body.

When a frog egg hatches,
a tadpole pops out.

Pop, pop, pop!

The black dots on this plant
are frog eggs.

This big frog came from a small egg.

www.harcourt.com

First Green Light Readers edition 2001
Green Light Readers is a trademark of Harcourt, Inc.,
registered in the United States of America and/or other jurisdictions.

Library of Congress Cataloging-in-Publication Data
Vern, Alex.
Where do frogs come from?/by Alex Vern.
p. cm.
"Green Light Readers."
1. Frogs—Development—Juvenile literature. [1. Tadpoles. 2. Frogs.]
I. Title. II. Series.
QL668.E2V47 2001
[E]—dc21   2001001481
ISBN 0-15-216304-2
ISBN 0-15-216296-8 (pb)

A C E G H F D B
A C E G H F D B (pb)

Where Do Frogs Come From?

Alex Vern

Green Light Readers
Harcourt, Inc.
San Diego   New York   London

Where Do **Frogs** Come From?

Green Light Readers

For the new reader who's ready to GO!

Amazing adventures await every young child who is eager to read.

Green Light Readers encourage children to explore, to imagine, and to grow through books. Created for beginning readers at two levels of skill, these lively illustrated stories have been carefully developed to reinforce reading basics taught at school and to make reading a fun and rewarding experience for children and grown-ups to share outside the classroom.

The grades and ages within each skill level are general guidelines only, and books included in both levels may feature any or all of the bulleted characteristics. When choosing a book for a new reader, remember that every child progresses at his or her own pace—be patient and supportive as the magic of reading takes hold.

1 **Buckle up!**
Kindergarten–Grade 1: Developing reading skills, ages 5–7
  • Short, simple stories • Fully illustrated • Familiar objects and situations
  • Playful rhythms • Spoken language patterns of children
  • Rhymes and repeated phrases • Strong link between text and art

2 **Start the engine!**
Grades 1–2: Reading with help, ages 6–8
  • Longer stories, including nonfiction • Short chapters
  • Generously illustrated • Less-familiar situations
  • More fully developed characters • Creative language, including dialogue
  • More subtle link between text and art

Green Light Readers incorporate characteristics detailed in the Reading Recovery model used by educators to assess the readability of texts through the end of first grade. Guidelines for reading levels for these readers have been developed with assistance from Mary Lou Meerson. An educational consultant, Ms. Meerson has been a classroom teacher, a language arts coordinator, an elementary school principal, and a university professor.

Published in collaboration with Harcourt School Publishers